MW01254004

Ninety-nine: Lost, Confused, and Found

M.S. Bernardo

Also by M.S. Bernardo

Ninety-nine: a beautiful chaos

Ninety-nine: Lost, Confused, and Found

M.S. Bernardo

Copyright © 2022 M.S. Bernardo

Cover Design by Angelo Bernardo

Published by M.S. Bernardo

ISBN 978 – 1 – 7773489 – 1 – 5

First Edition September 2022

Ninety-nine: Lost, Confused, and Found

For my parents, my brothers, and my sister,

thank you for keeping the hope in me stay alive.

M.S. Bernardo

CONTENTS

Lost

Ninety-nine: Lost, Confused, and Found

M.S. Bernardo

LOST

M.S. Bernardo

Ninety-nine: Lost, Confused, and Found

What can I do?

The harsh words I hear,
Will it ever go away?
How long do I have to bear?
I keep losing my days.

What do they know about me?
Their words doesn't stop.
I wonder what they see,
They prevent me from the top.

What wrong have I done?
They keep hurting me.
No matter how much I run,
Why can't they just let me be?

Their words corner me,
I act as if it doesn't matter,
But that's all I get to see,
I want to feel better.

Why do they satisfy themselves like that?
Why does my pain make them so happy?
I wonder, why are they so glad,
That I'm feeling this crappy?

What can I do to escape their views?
They don't even know me.

M.S. Bernardo

Why do I see their words so true?
I want to be free.

Can Heaven see?

My mind's gone with the wind,
Dancing through and free,
Hand in hand with destiny,
Can Heaven see?

Am I the rebel?
Or am I the angel?
Was I the one who fell?
All for the stories I'd like to tell.

Word after word,
I'm drowning in this chaos of a world,
Word after word,
I'm long gone from the world.

Free in a prison I made,
Maybe my soul can never be saved.
Maybe Heaven gave up on coming to my aid,
Maybe all I am, is afraid.

M.S. Bernardo

My thoughts

The thoughts inside my head are in chaos,
Like someone broke out a fire,
And they struggle to get across,
The bridge created by the liar.

They're stuck where they are,
They make my head hurt,
The light's getting too far,
Now my heart's on alert.

Pain and sorrow came from nowhere,
Hope's gone on vacation.
Now my thoughts are in despair,
Pointing at each other for accusation.

Can they be saved from each other?
I'm trying to call hope to come back,
But hope cannot be bothered,
My thoughts burned to black.

Me who loves me

Is there anyone who can hear me?
Even around others I'm lonely.
The words of someone trying to be free,
I still walk towards it slowly.

The reflection of myself,
Since when did it become so strange?
It feels as if I'm standing on the edge,
How much have I really changed?

Who am I trying to please?
Why can't I accept myself?
I keep feeling the cold harsh breeze,
Where are the words I once pledged?

I want to be a me who loves me,
Why can't I do that?
Why can't I feel the peace?
Why do I only pretend to laugh?

Someday it'll be okay,
Can someone please tell me those words?
Even if I never find my own way,
Don't I still belong in this world?

How much longer must I suffer?
Why am I my worst enemy?

M.S. Bernardo

I only believed this is making me tougher,
But I keep on losing mentally.

Can I look at myself with love again?
Can I smile at myself someday?
I can only ask the questions of when,
When will I be okay?

I still cannot tell

I'm in conflict with my thoughts,
Should I fight it or should I give in?
Sleepless nights it have brought,
This is how my fights have been.

Weighing what's lost and what I gain,
Still, I am afraid.
I stand under this chaos of pain,
My decisions haven't been made.

Should I choose a life with struggles?
Or should I choose a life with no smile?
Why am I stuck in this endless battle?
For what reason do I stand trial?

Which way would my heart choose?
I still cannot tell.
Time passing is time I lose,
This is where my heart dwells.

M.S. Bernardo

Words of no one

People like to criticize,
Just for conversation,
But they don't realize,
They're no better creation.

I became scared of their words,
I hid myself in my room,
I'm lost inside my own world,
I created my own doom.

"I'll listen to your worries,"
The words of no one,
Even if it gets blurry,
Their words don't stay gone.

No one saw behind my mask,
I want to smile sincerely too,
Only if they bothered to ask,
Maybe I could've been true.

"I'm sorry,"
The words of no one,
Even if you worry,
You won't ever stay gone.

Could it have been any different?
I wish it could be,

Ninety-nine: Lost, Confused, and Found

If only they hear what their words sent,
Then they would see.

"It's okay not to be okay,"
The words of no one,
Even if you keep losing your way,
You won't ever be gone.

When did my words became like theirs?
They're still the ones holding the gun,
I still hear it like a curse,
If only they could see me as someone.

M.S. Bernardo

Depression

I stand in front of you,
Look me in the eyes,
I want to know if you're true,
Perhaps, a lie?

Stuck in between four walls,
Surrounded by white,
I can hear your voice calls,
A darkness within the light.

You're here, aren't you?
I knew you would be.
They tell me you're not true,
But they just don't see.

I didn't lose my mind,
I'm as real as you.
In the corner, you'll always find,
I knew as my heart always knew.

I don't like it this way

I don't like it this way,
My life, I mean,
Struggling every day,
I don't want to be seen.

Breaking my body for my needs,
Breaking my soul for my heart,
This world overflowing with greed,
Why is being human so hard?

I can't afford being ill,
I can't afford my own dreams,
I'm suffering as I stand so still,
My head filled up with my screams.

How should I make this work out?
How can I pull life onto my side?
My voice drowned by my own doubts,
My life so long had died.

M.S. Bernardo

God help me be better

I clasp my hands together,
Closed my eyes and prayed,
"God help me be better,
I'm tired of being afraid.

I want to live my life,
Without the shadows on my back.
Can I get rid of that knife?
Will reality halt its attack?

Because I believe there's also a chance for me,
Please help me be stronger.
My heart and mind so long not free,
I know my life can get better.

But the words are long gone,
God please give me another chance.
Tirelessly I will run towards your command,
Please save me, save me from life's dance."

The way of fears

I want this to be happy,
But I'm afraid it'll be sad.
Can these words be at all pretty?
I'm afraid they're bad.

To end my note with tears,
I hope to begin again.
Isn't that the way of fears?
Pain and doubt became my friends.

All these broken promises I made,
Tomorrow will only add more.
Pain from my own blade,
Why can't we ever go back to before?

It asks for too much

This waiting game is killing me,
But I know what I want,
I want to feel alive and free,
But I can't stand up to life's command.

It asks for too much,
I don't want to give up my time,
My own breath I can't even catch,
Why is living a crime?

Why do I feel so guilty?
What did I do wrong?
I'm my own beauty,
I'm my own beautiful song.

But the world doesn't want me,
It asks for too much,
Preventing me from breaking free,
It stole hope's graceful touch.

Pretending

I'm keeping it together,
Like I'm not losing my mind,
Hoping I'll get better,
Pretending like everything's fine,

Wondering why I'm this way,
Silently I let my pain grow,
I want all of it to go away,
Someone, please take away my sorrows.

But I smile, because I'm fine,
I laugh, though I want to cry,
I am losing my mind,
But I might get better if I try,

Still, my mind's convinced I won't ever heal,
That life is meant to be sorrow and tears,
That soon, death will make its steal,
But death, is not what I fear.

M.S. Bernardo

Gone far

I wrote my heart out,
But it wasn't enough.
My mind drowning in doubts,
But I thought I was tough.

Now I can't even cry,
And it's so hard,
I do my best and try,
But I can no longer feel my heart.

Is it so broken that it can't smile?
I don't remember how I got here.
And as it turns out, my reality is a lie,
My only hope disappears.

Gone far, far away,
Too far for my heart.
Now I'm covered with words I won't say,
My mind is tearing me apart.

This life of a freezing breeze

Is this life?
I don't know anything.
Am I even really alive?
Sometimes, I feel everything.

Is it normal?
To feel so shallow at times,
To be in so much denial,
Is feeling all these a crime?

What does it mean to be human?
What does it mean to live?
I've got nothing, no plans,
But everything for this heart to grieve.

I've got no idea how to be in peace,
Too much chaos up in my head,
This life of a freezing breeze,
This is the life I've always dread.

M.S. Bernardo

I pretend my heart is free

I carry with me
Secrets of my heart
Stories the world won't see
Hidden within my art

But there's no one who'll believe
Not even my false soul
This heart of mine only knows how to grieve
Losing sight of my goal

I wonder if it's supposed to be like that
But I've got no idea of how it's supposed to be
So in the corner of my heart so sad
I pretend my heart is free

Maybe then I'll be spared
Even these lies carry my truth
But for life that couldn't be more prepared
On my own heart I stood

Behind it all

The typical words I say,
I'm still scared.
Even though I act so brave,
I'm still unprepared.

No matter how much I say I'm okay,
Time chases me from behind.
Even though I'm going the right way,
I still feel confined.

The voice of my dream,
Will the world listen?
I know what exactly it means,
But I doubt it again.

Courage is all I need,
That's what I always say.
But can I really succeed,
Even when I keep on being swayed?

The comforting words I let in,
Still the fear lives in my head.
Even after I win,
I keep worrying about what's ahead.

I advice others to live in the moment,
I can't even do it myself.

M.S. Bernardo

With that kind of resentment,
I'm only pretending to have the strength.

Time will fix everything,
But what if it doesn't?
What if I break my wings?
What if I get lost again?

Even though I still have the hope,
I can't help but be scared.
I'm still tied to that rope,
Can I still be repaired?

Tomorrow I'll be fine

I remember my painful yesterday,
Today, I fell again.
Sometimes I can't help but lose my way,
Once again, today is filled with pain.

Until when will I suffer from this?
Until when will this live inside me?
I feel like there's so many I'll miss,
Because the yesterday is all I see.

I want to smile without watching my shadows,
I don't want to be scared of myself,
How can life feel this shallow?
Is this really my best?

Is healing even real?
Sometimes I can't help but wonder.
From me the pain continues to steal,
Why is my reflection her?

I want to feel better,
I'm sure tomorrow I'll be fine.
But what if it won't get brighter?
Is this really the end of the line?

Is there no more hope for me?
What about my heart?

M.S. Bernardo

Did I once again lose the key?
What about my art?

Within confusion

I'm not proud of who I used to be,
And I'm scared of who I'll become,
Why am I scared of me?
When did life became so numb?

I get hurt by my own words,
I'm scared of how I feel,
Is everyone like this in the world?
Is it really possible to heal?

Why are the lies easier to believe?
Who is to blame for all of these?
Why are the lies better to receive?
In what way must we resist?

How can I exist truly within this confusion?
Is there an answer anywhere?
Maybe if I live a life of illusion,
Then maybe, I won't be in so much despair.

M.S. Bernardo

My existence

It doesn't make sense,
My existence,
Innocent eyes,
I drowned under lies,

My own mostly,
That's what made me so lonely,
I separated from the crowd,
My heart crying under the gray cloud,

I could've been saved,
But I wasn't too brave,
So I remained in silence,
Questioning my own existence.

Before the sun I needed most,
I became the crying ghost,
Haunting my own heart,
Letting my world fall apart.

Someone's smile

Everyone's living so busily,
Why are we living in a rush?
I don't even know why it feels empty,
I feel like I'm living like a trash.

Will it always be like this?
Pretending to be happy.
Do we even really exist?
Why does it feel so heavy?

My tears that won't even come out,
Because someone might notice.
How can silence be so loud?
I don't want their diagnosis.

I know I'm sick,
But I don't want to admit it.
I just have to make my smile thick,
I don't want them to notice.

Can't you see it?
What's behind someone's smile?
No one wants to admit,
Life is nothing but a failed trial.

I don't want to feel empty anymore,
But will it even really get better?

M.S. Bernardo

How long exactly is this war?
Maybe this is my last letter.

If it is,
Will it all turn out okay?
I definitely won't miss this,
Maybe that is my way.

Drowning in reset

I wish to move forward,
But can't take the step,
Why is this so hard?
Drowning in reset.

Begin again,
That's the way,
Take your hold on your pen,
And write out the day.

But I'm always starting and ending,
I've got no in between,
The reason my heart should be mending,
So much for the love within.

I'm frustrated but don't know what to do,
I'm tired but can't give up,
So I guess once again, I'm starting anew,
Following an empty map.

M.S. Bernardo

Will I be able to overcome it?

I had a dream last night
People cornered me with bad words
Even though it shines so bright
The light disappeared within the words I heard

It's a fact: not everyone will like
The words I continue to lay out
But it still makes me sigh
Once again, I'm covered in doubts

Because I write these words from my heart
I continue to get hurt
Even though I give my all for my art
I still get cursed

That dream that felt so real
Will I be able to overcome it?
Will I ever get to heal?
Once again I'm covered with fears.

Ninety-nine: Lost, Confused, and Found

Different days

I'm living differently from yesterday,
Not many things changed.
Unlike yesterday, today feels gray,
But it doesn't feel that strange.

As if it happens every day,
Why am I having a hard time again?
Again it's the same words I say,
"It'll all be okay once I hold the pen."

But even dreamers get tired,
And I wonder if I'm feeling this too fast.
Even when writing stays on my side,
I always wonder how long it'll last.

No matter how much I promise,
Of course, I'll get bad days like today.
Even when I know it's something I'll miss,
I still get lost on my way.

But I'll be fine,
Because I have to be.
But just because I claim this mine,
Doesn't mean I'll always see.

M.S. Bernardo

Show me

Save me from desperation,
Lay me an inspiration,
Take away the war inside,
Show me the eyes that still hide.

Wipe away my tears,
Stolen dreams by my fears,
Golden smile from the past,
The future does not last.

And I don't know what to make of that,
All this living, it makes me sad,
To try but fulfill nothing,
For what reason am I smiling?

Will I find out soon enough?
I miss the sound of my own laugh.
Show me the reasons I've lost,
Show me the mercy of my loss.

Ninety-nine: Lost, Confused, and Found

Love for me

There's so much love in my heart,
Why isn't there any for myself?
Just getting by became so hard,
Is pain something I've always felt?

There's a chaos in my head,
I don't even know where it came from.
Every day I get stuck on my bed,
No, I don't want to feel numb.

Why does it only get worse?
I'm trying hard to be okay.
Is this someone's curse?
I'll get out of your way.

Tomorrow please give me back my hope,
Isn't there some love I have for me?
Cut away this tight rope,
Where is the real me I can't see?

Have I given it all away?
I meant the every ounce of love in my heart.
Why does my mind make me feel so gray?
Why am I tearing myself apart?

Surely I'll get better, right?
Life can't possibly be this tragic.

M.S. Bernardo

Oh heavens, show me some light,
Can't you grant me some magic?

Pressure of today

No matter how much I try,
Why does it feel the same?
Can I really fly?
What if I end up in shame?

Why did I get these thoughts again?
But yesterday was okay.
Even when I'm still holding the pen,
Why is it so hard to see the way?

I keep planning it out,
I don't even know what tomorrow holds.
I can't even say what this is about,
Is life really this cold?

Knowing that we live in limited time,
Why am I only trying so hard?
I keep worrying about the climb,
Maybe I'm forgetting what's in my heart.

I don't want to feel like this,
But I keep getting desperate.
There's so much I already missed,
Why do I keep going back to this state?

Will this feeling disappear one day?
Why can't I feel satisfied?

M.S. Bernardo

There's so many words I want to say,
But it feels as if those words have already died.

I'm sorry to who I was yesterday,
And I'm sorry to who I'll be tomorrow.
I keep bringing you under a sky so gray,
I'm only filling up your sorrows.

I hope someday it'll all really be okay,
I wish I can sincerely promise that it will be.
I just wish I won't ever again lose my way,
After all, isn't life also for me?

Smiling through

I don't want to worry anyone else,
Why am I such a mess?
Pretending everything's okay,
Just so I won't be in their way.

I'm trying hard,
Because I want to please my heart,
I'm giving it my best,
But somehow can't let myself rest.

I realized someone happy might not be,
There's a lot we don't see,
Are we all just smiling through?
How much of us is actually true?

Of course everyone's got it hard,
Everyone's got a story in their heart,
But that doesn't mean mine don't matter,
I can no longer push my pain for later.

If only I can accept this life,
But I end up only accepting the lie,
So how can I possibly feel better?
Will I see my truth after this letter?

Living under the blazing sun,
I know hard days will always come,

M.S. Bernardo

But no one told me it's okay to cry,
I did nothing but give my best to try.

Am I being dramatic?
When life keeps being this realistic?
Life still makes me wonder,
But all I feel is its thunder.

But I know no situation is permanent,
So I still feel determined,
That someday I'll understand,
That life can also be grand.

That this won't last,
Because life's too vast,
But as life's always a question,
I will have to make a decision.

Either I control it,
And let pain the one I greet,
Or I take control of me,
And let myself fly free.

Still, I don't know if I'll be better,
But I know I want to be greater,
For myself that I once killed,
I won't live a life so completely sealed.

I'll still put on a smile and not a frown,

Ninety-nine: Lost, Confused, and Found

Even when it's hard and I'm beaten down,
So even though I am far too tired,
I still have the hope that remains as my guide.

M.S. Bernardo

The person that is me

A day goes by,
Nothing's changed.
Living as I lie,
I feel so strange.

Take a look around,
Everything's busy.
Looking for my own crown,
Why do I feel so guilty?

Breathing with strength,
I can't recognize myself.
The future I chose to forget,
How can I think that was the best?

Please look at me,
Give me back all that's been lost,
Let me see the person I need to see,
I'm the one I need most.

The person who stands before my eyes,
That person who is me,
Please let go of your heart's lies,
Please give me back my key.

For the tomorrow I wish to be bright,
Please release me.

Ninety-nine: Lost, Confused, and Found

To once again open my sight,
You've got to set me free.

M.S. Bernardo

Dear soul in me

I carry a soul in me,
She wants to fly away,
So many words she wants to say,
Beautifully, she wants to stay.

A soul that longs to be free,
She longs to be brave,
In a world that won't give half of what she gave,
Let her shine before she reaches her grave.

Can't you see?
A human soul so fragile to live,
So empty, she wants to leave,
But so pure not to let anyone grieve.

Get well, dear soul in me,
We don't need the world to look,
Just you and me and the bait on life's hook,
We're the ones to finish our beautiful book.

Confused

M.S. Bernardo

I hope one day, I'll be able to get across

I've always wondered how tomorrow is like,
I wonder if it's really worth the hike.
If my dreams really would come true,
If I'll really get that kind of view.

Will I even really understand life?
Can I really get rid of my own knife?
I'm not even sure if I'm giving my best,
Why does it feel like all I do is rest?

Tomorrow, will I be able to breathe?
Can I show everything I hid underneath?
I wonder if life really would get better,
If for me, there's really something greater.

I wonder if I'm blindly falling in a trap,
I can't even see my own heart's map.
I wonder if all my efforts will breed something,
Do I really have something to bring?

I believe everyone's special,
But do I really have the potential?
There's a bigger life that I want,
But what if it becomes a wish I cannot grant?

If it's like that, will I be able to get myself
through?

M.S. Bernardo

If it's like that, can I remain true?
Will I be able to forgive myself if it comes to that?
Will I be okay if life happens so fast?

I push myself to stay hopeful,
Maybe one day I'll really be successful.
But what if I'm just plainly being greedy,
For that answer, I'm not ready.

Are these questions useless to ask?
Maybe I should just focus on the task.
But I can't help but get these thoughts,
I hope one day, I'll be able to get across.

I am me

There's a dark cloud in my head,
I'm still awake on my bed.
Maybe if I wake up dead,
I'll remember all the words I never said.

But life's too cruel to let us be,
It makes us feel we're never free,
It shows us memories we don't need to see,
I keep forgetting, I am me.

The girl who dreams in vain,
The girl who may be insane,
Devastated under the rain,
But know, she can never be contained.

So she keeps pushing against destiny,
She's choosing her own harmony,
Forget everything about the money,
We don't need the company.

I'll forever stay as me,
That's the only way for me to be free.
Only if the world could let me be,
But purpose, it cannot see.

M.S. Bernardo

Restless

Some nights are like this,
I feel so restless.
This feeling that can't be missed,
It turns my head into a mess.

If I don't write,
I won't be able to sleep.
But not sleeping isn't right,
The passion slowly creeps in.

I don't even know where to start,
I don't know what to write,
I slowly search the words from my heart,
Because I always say writing is right.

I tightly hold the pen,
My mind suddenly goes blank.
I'm trying to try again,
But there's nothing in my word bank.

So I take a deep breath,
I have to write something.
I should be sleeping instead,
But my mind isn't done ringing.

I stare at the blank page,
Where did the words go?

Ninety-nine: Lost, Confused, and Found

I'm slowly turning to rage,
The words really won't flow.

Will I be able to sleep tonight?
I don't know.
But the page is still white,
My mind's working too slow.

With no thoughts,
I'm just itching to write.
But now I'm in distraught,
Because my eyes wants to say good night.

M.S. Bernardo

Forever trap

Wanders eternally,
Meeting of eternity,
At peace finally,
Still not my reality,

Forever's long gone,
Sight of a bright sun,
Saved by the Son,
Death by a man,

Heaven's too far,
Hell will be my scar,
My soul once a star,
Lost sound of the guitar,

Dear angel, have you given up?
I know, pain doesn't stop,
My soul can't be lifted to the top,
My soul, forever trap.

Lavenders on my grave

As bright as yellow
As sad as blue
Meet me tomorrow
I'll show you what's true

As fierce as red
Fresh like green
Not yet dead
Away from what we've seen

Love me like I'm gone
Then maybe happy we'll be
Like the moon loves the sun
You've got to set me free

Lavenders on my grave
Colorful will the death I'll have
Soul longs to be brave
Be as free as a dove

Gone like a winter storm
You'll remember me
Tomorrow hope is born
Only if you'll let it be

Goodbye my love
Greetings to yesterday

M.S. Bernardo

I'll be flying high above
I'm sorry I couldn't stay

What should I write about?

I sit here blankly,
I'm waiting for the words to escape.
Words with no accuracy,
These words come in no shape.

My eyes are lost,
My mind in wonder,
Emptiness I can't get across,
My mind doesn't seem to bother.

Will it be like this all night?
Will I be able to get a word out?
Soon I'll turn off the light,
What should I write about?

Time could no longer wait,
My eyes long for its sleep.
Maybe tomorrow will be differently great,
I'll search the words I've hidden deep.

M.S. Bernardo

The wind of when I was young

I remember the wind of when I was young,
The words of its tongue,
"Dear little girl, you'll make it far.
Dear little girl, you're a star."

But that wind went away,
I long to feel it again,
To hear the words it'll say,
To feel the memories that remains.

Will it come back for me?
The wind of when I was young,
The wind that opened my eyes to see,
The wind that once sung.

Will life be merciful enough?
I wish it would be.
I want to hear the wind that made me tough,
The wind that made me see.

Pink and White

What did the monsters want from me?
What did you let me see?
Was that really necessary?
Why was I not free?

Pink on my left,
White on my right,
How can I forget?
I also saw the light.

I kept running away,
But they kept finding me.
I thought I won't again see the day,
But you handed me the key.

I should say thank you,
But I want to understand.
Was that dream really true?
Was that another land?

You saved me,
I still don't understand why.
You broke me free,
Then I saw you fly.

They might come back,
But I'll have the pink and white.

M.S. Bernardo

If ever they once again attack,
I know you'll help me fight.

Ninety-nine: Lost, Confused, and Found

I'm too young

I'm too young for my body to break
I'm too young to put everything at stake
But as life brought me to fate
All I can do is simply wait

Hoping my days become for the better
And no more regrets for later
That someday, I will be my own
No longer feeling so alone

I'm too young for these thoughts
But life doesn't choose who to put in distraught
Life picks on you when you resist
That's the way it owns the way we exist

But I'm hopeful for better days
As I've always say
I'm too young to break
But too old for fate

M.S. Bernardo

Stories

Am I too much in my head?
Should I stay behind instead?
Should I let the stories go?
What of my tomorrow?

Maybe I am insane,
Fighting myself in vain,
But I can at least say that I'm my own,
Hurting myself with my own stone.

I avoided what they threw,
Chose my own rocks of hue,
After all, I'm the one who gets to live,
I must choose what I can give.

Stories of hello and farewell,
There's so much stories I want to tell,
That's why I fight myself and the world,
I fight for myself and my words.

Garden full of thorns

In a garden full of thorns,
I found love in my heart.
In a world once I was born,
Taught me a love so hard.

What was meant for me,
I cannot give.
Freedom I refused to see,
Because of how others lived.

And painfully I exist,
But beautifully I remain,
Still I resist,
Only to play their game.

But in a garden full of thorns,
I will stand out.
For a life I still mourn,
I gather my voice to shout.

I am still beautiful,
This love is for me,
But quietly the pain still pull,
Maybe I'm never really free.

M.S. Bernardo

Will I really glow?

Some people might think I'm crazy,
Well, I could be.
It's not that bad to be me,
That's something I now see.

The future I'm creating,
I'm spreading my wings.
There's still some I have to bring,
But right now I'm just waiting.

But patience can run out too,
That's something I recently knew.
The wind of yesterday already blew,
Tomorrow will be a different view.

But how far is that tomorrow?
Will it really clear all of my sorrows?
I believe on my continuous growth,
But I wonder if I'll really glow.

See you on that day

How are you feeling?
I hope you're okay.
Even though you found the meaning,
I know you still have some to say.

I'm okay,
You don't have to worry.
I'm happy we stayed,
So stop being sorry.

Let go of what hurts,
I'm doing the same.
Time we can't reverse,
Stop taking the blame.

Some of them will understand,
But not everyone.
I'm still holding your hand,
Our life finally began.

I'm crying tears of joy,
I'm okay.
This life we should enjoy,
See you on that day.

M.S. Bernardo

Serenity

Stay true to your heart
Even when it's hard
Rest yourself from time to time
Especially when you're not feeling fine
Never will I take you for granted
I believe in those words I said
Tomorrow the peace will be achieved
You'll be the one I won't ever deceive

Rest day

You've been giving it your best,
Why don't you rest today?
In life, you don't always have to be stressed,
It's also okay if you're a bit delayed.

It's not like you do it every time,
Give yourself a break,
Resting isn't a crime,
Resting is also for your sake.

Don't overdo everything,
You don't have to,
Don't break your wings,
Or else you might lose the view.

Let yourself breathe,
Don't lose your heart,
Life will never feel complete,
Even if you try really hard.

So let yourself rest,
Let yourself breathe,
Sometimes it's for the best,
Stopping for a moment isn't defeat.

M.S. Bernardo

In the face of life

I'm not scared of life,
I'm scared I'll waste it.
I'm not scared of being alive,
But I'm scared I might not commit.

It's not the troubles that worries me,
It's everything perfect that does.
I can live with pain, you see,
But I can't live with such rush.

I worry when things fall into place,
I feel like I did something wrong.
I've become worried of my own face,
I lost what it means to be strong.

But still, in the face of life, I am trying.
That's at least worth something. It's gotta be.
Maybe someday I'll see myself flying,
That would be a sight I'd love to see.

Learning to love myself

No one taught me,
That life happens unexpectedly.
Pain made me see,
That life doesn't let you exist quietly.

Hiding under a smile,
I'm learning to love myself.
Living can be quite fatal,
I'm just another victim of theft.

The words I couldn't say,
I still try to figure out myself.
Looking around for my own way,
Should I turn right or to the left?

There were only two ways in front of me,
Why couldn't I see the rest?
I want to let myself be,
Why is life just full of tests?

I'm hoping for a better tomorrow,
I want to love myself,
So that whichever way I go,
I won't ever come to regret.

M.S. Bernardo

Perfectly not perfect

A child who grows,
Learning what life really is,
Time filled with sorrows,
Showing us everything we missed.

Wanting to be perfect,
Trying everything at hand,
Until no heart is left,
There's no one who understand.

Where is life taking us?
Am I still important?
Many things we can't discuss,
Why do we only have wishes we can't grant?

Is it a sin to be me?
Because I'm perfectly not perfect?
My heart you won't even see,
But it's mine to protect.

So I'll fight for myself,
There's no one who'll do it.
Even if in the end there's only me left,
Living as someone else is a sin I won't commit.

Because I'm perfectly not perfect,
I'm learning to love every ounce of me.

Ninety-nine: Lost, Confused, and Found

It's my own self I shouldn't neglect,
It's me who I need to set free.

M.S. Bernardo

Burden of a dream

The burden of a dream,
The fear that it's not real,
That maybe it's just a lie,
Something to wish for before we die.

What if it's just another false hope?
What if it's tied to that rope?
What if I later change my mind?
Even now, I look for a sign.

I know this is for me,
But what if there's something I can't see?
Because of the words "be realistic"
I'm scared I'll end up with the wrong pick.

The happy me who writes,
Still fighting for that light.
Or the scared me who worries,
With a future so blurry.

What's not real about my dream?
You don't know how I feel.
Even though I know this is right,
I'm scared of what might.

This world asks for too much,
I won't ever lose my touch.

Ninety-nine: Lost, Confused, and Found

The dream I'm still fighting for,
I'll make sure you'll hear my loud roar.

M.S. Bernardo

Found

M.S. Bernardo

My heart is free

Complications of the heart,
My thoughts had fallen apart,
Live with the world's truthful lies,
They told me I can never rise.

So I believed their words,
I mean, who am I in this world?
But persistence opened my eyes,
I also deserve the golden prize.

A combination of smile and tears,
I am bravely fighting my fears.
I am stronger than you make of me,
Because I decided my heart is free.

And one day, the angels will shine their light,
Upon me who took courage for the flight.
And even then, I will write,
Still hoping one day, life's no longer a fight.

M.S. Bernardo

Right words in a made up world

I'm a writer without the right words,
I'm a girl living in a made up world,
I wonder if tomorrow I'll be the same,
Will I leave as soon as I came?

My heart that was pure,
Tainted with the belief there is a cure,
For the sickness this world suffers from,
But I'm afraid, the cure is long gone.

But if by chance I find the right words,
Then it'll become real, my made up world,
Then I'll be the girl who found her hope,
I'll be the girl who broke free from life's rope,

I'll be the girl who didn't give up,
Maybe the one who reaches the top,
But that kind of hope seems too far,
Having that hope sounds too bizarre,

But I do want to find the right words,
I want to find my made up world,
I have hope there's some light for me,
I just have to keep my eyes open to see,

And I'll see it, maybe,
My cure is hidden somewhere in my heart,

Ninety-nine: Lost, Confused, and Found

But right now I've not got the ability,
Still, I'll try even though it's hard.

M.S. Bernardo

Its worth

I stare at it blankly,
I'm scared of what I'll write.
My words take me cruelly,
But I know they're right.

These words of pain,
Makes peace with my heart,
Admiring the rain,
From the first word I'll start.

Maybe I'll write about me,
Or maybe about you,
Then my soul would see,
How this poem grew.

It'll be something of mine,
I'll be proud of every word.
Even when the fear still shines,
Wouldn't I still feel its worth?

I love who I am

I love who I am,
That's mostly right.
Listening to words I once sang,
I'm running towards my own light.

Regrets I've come face to face with,
Finally, my smile is true.
Dreams I still greet,
Happy to say I got through.

Still, the questions challenge me,
But I've come to love my heart,
Because I know who I can be,
I'll show you my precious art.

These words that's now my strength,
But I know I can still fall,
Still, imagine the pleasure my heart gets,
I'm breaking down my own wall.

M.S. Bernardo

She's not dead yet

A life that will be,
She's a lot like the sea,
Beautiful but deadly,
Still, I hope she's happy.

A little girl full of smile,
But soon, she will die,
Her life of trials,
I wish to see her fly.

She's not dead yet,
But as life was met,
So will be death,
That's what we'll all get.

But she needs to be alive,
Her dreams still needs to arrive,
With my heart and soul I strive,
I want her badly to survive.

Ninety-nine: Lost, Confused, and Found

Forest of dreams

In the forest of dreams,
I tripped and fell,
The deafening silent screams,
I've got stories to tell.

The words flowed with my blood,
The smile and tears came all at once,
My mind drowning in its own flood,
The trees offer me a hand of chance.

My heart was afraid,
But I reached out towards the branch,
A decision was made,
The world will feel my heart's punch.

Both chaos and peace,
My heart rests here in the forest of dreams,
About time to say my piece,
Hear, hear, my heart's hopeful scream.

M.S. Bernardo

Lame poetry

My heart's restless,
I need to write.
Is it a curse to be such a mess?
But this feels right.

What should I do to calm my heart?
But the chaos feels familiar.
I struggle towards my art,
I struggle for my dream's too far.

Words that rhymes like these,
Sometimes it carries no beauty,
But no words will be missed,
Lame poetry also makes me happy.

So I write and I write,
I live with the chaos of my heart,
To be a mess feels too right,
I'm the chaos of my art.

Ninety-nine: Lost, Confused, and Found

Pen

I pick up the pen,
I'm ready.
I'm trying again,
Keeping it steady.

Words of my world,
I'm trying to shine,
Like a star of words,
I'm making it mine.

I'll fall, and fall again,
But I'll get up just as fast,
Building a future with a pen,
Hoping the words will last.

As I keep on going,
My pen keeps on writing,
As much as I can go on living,
I will keep on trying.

M.S. Bernardo

All I wish for

We'll find what's ours,
All in due time.
Blooming with power,
Then we'll learn to shine.

Simple life while smiling,
That's all I wish for.
My heart still dreaming,
I'm opening a new door.

I'll be the woman I dreamed of,
I'll be the child I once lost,
Towards my dreams I'm off,
Measuring the weight of cost.

I'll be in pain if I stay still,
So I give it my all for my dreams.
I refused the time passing to kill,
I've learned to accept life by my own means.

Someday, I hope I can see

I started writing a long time ago,
Even before I knew I wanted to be a writer.
I continued on with that flow,
I did it to be better.

Now, a while has gone,
I'm still writing my heart out.
I sleep at the rise of the sun,
My own words kill my doubts.

Someday, when I die,
I will be proud of how I lived my life.
Because I learned to let go of my lies,
And my pen became my knife.

As sharp as it can be,
My words defended my heart.
Someday, I hope I can see,
What would become of my art.

M.S. Bernardo

We survived

They burned us alive,
All those years back,
Still, we survived,
Distanced from their attack.

But we remember,
How they silenced us,
Alive for the better,
Our existence will last.

Our magic hasn't faded to dust,
Our hearts have been lifted up,
Even when blinded by a broken trust,
My magic never stopped.

I survived their flames,
I'm alive today,
I'll survive all their shameless blames,
My magic never went away.

I'm taking my time

It seems that I'm taking my time,
As I should.
What I'm doing isn't a crime,
This is good.

Because there are thoughts I can't understand,
And I'm just doing my best,
Even for a dream I really want,
I still need to rest.

Hoping someday it'll get better,
Hoping I'll feel lighter,
Maybe someday with another letter,
I'll be a better fighter.

M.S. Bernardo

You're beautiful, little girl

You're beautiful, little girl,
But they'll tell you otherwise,
Then they'll tell you an advice,
That will only delay your rise.

They'll give you false hope,
All covered with their lies,
And while your own heart dies,
They'll only silent down your cries.

I hope you find courage to turn away,
Find your own belief within your heart.
I wish you'll find yourself within your soul's art,
Don't let them completely tear you apart.

You're beautiful, little girl,
I hope you'll find your own way,
I hope you find the words you want to say,
And I hope it'll be in peace your soul will lay.

A dream that'll come true

I lose track of time,
But I like it.
Someday, maybe I'll shine,
That's a future I'll greet.

Greedy with dreams,
I'm not ashamed anymore.
Listen to the chaos of my screams,
My wings will soar.

Though right now,
I'm all just words,
But hear my vow,
My name will be known in the world.

You'll know me,
And I'll thank you,
That's a dream I see,
A dream that'll come true.

M.S. Bernardo

Dream chaser

As a kid I thought of many possibilities,
Still I felt limited.
One by one, life only became about
responsibilities,
My dreams became something prohibited.

I grew up like an empty shell,
Thinking about a future I didn't know.
I locked myself in my own cell,
Because I thought I didn't have anything to show.

Once I woke up and realized I was wrong,
I pulled myself out of that darkness.
Even though the way ahead seemed so long,
It's better than any kind of empty success.

I didn't want to be like them,
That made me different in their eyes.
But I needed to start again,
I couldn't go back to their lies.

I want to write,
For as long as my heart wants.
For me, this is what's right,
No matter their response.

I just wished they'd understand,

Ninety-nine: Lost, Confused, and Found

Not everyone goes down the same path.
They couldn't even offer me a hand,
They didn't bother to ask.

All they saw was the impossible dreams I had,
Why couldn't they see this was for me?
But now, even if the whole world thinks I'm mad,
I won't ever change the dreams I see.

M.S. Bernardo

A dream and a chance

You're not given a dream
Without also being given a chance
So let out your deepest screams
And let your heart dance

Someday, it'll all be realized
But right now we must breathe
For the day that we do rise
We'll taste just how it can be sweet

Trust your heart and run
Run forward and fall
We exist with the shining sun
We're here to answer Heaven's call

So pick yourself up
It's all going to be okay
Doesn't matter if you end up on top
What matters is choosing your own way

Ninety-nine: Lost, Confused, and Found

I'll do as I promised Him

I remember when I used to hate the world,
The time when there was no hope in my heart,
A time when I couldn't find my words,
When even breathing was hard,

Feeling like I didn't deserve anything good,
I brought myself deeper,
Deeper than I should,
Hence my heart becoming bitter,

But I got through,
With a light from Heaven,
And as I became true,
Receiving what I've been given,

Hope filled my empty heart,
Dreams buried down my doubts,
I finally found my own art,
I found what my life's about,

And as I've been saved,
I'll offer my hand too,
Because He made me brave,
Showing me how to get through,

Words will be my way,
I'll do as I promised Him,

M.S. Bernardo

To fulfill all my remaining days,
Filled with my love for Him.

Life playing fair

I was scared at first,
To take the courageous step,
But I was overwhelmed with thirst,
So I went on ahead.

I felt nothing then I felt joy,
Then I remembered, I was afraid.
But I learned to play it, as if it's a toy,
And I enjoyed it enough for fear to fade.

And I made chances,
Miracles of my pen,
Through its ink the words dances,
And I'm willing to do it again.

I never would have thought,
Life knows how to play fair,
And it was I, the words had sought,
A fate life and I share.

M.S. Bernardo

Raise your voice

Raise your voice,
Make them listen.
You have a choice,
Remember your ambition.

It might be a little different,
They'll learn to accept.
Don't you dare prevent,
The dreams you've kept.

Show the world who you are,
Let's raise our voices.
Because we know we can go far,
It's all about choices.

So fast

Time's going by so fast,
Life's running not to last,
My heart fading into rust,
Yet my future is still vast.

Not sure where to run,
Hiding my pain from the sun,
Still I play along with the fun,
I am still my number one.

Living as much as my heart,
Not forgetting the way of art,
In a world that can hit so hard,
We still get our rewards.

And so fast we'll die,
So no use for us to lie,
Crying as we still try,
Hoping someday we'll fly.

M.S. Bernardo

Story's plot

I'm here,
Watch me grow.
It's clear,
I know I'll glow.

Watch me smile,
As I run towards my heart.
In my own style,
I'll show you my own art.

Whether it's great, or maybe not,
It's mine, and for that I am proud.
Living in my own story's plot,
I'm happy to live it out loud.

Because I finally believe in me,
And in what I can do,
So now I see,
My dreams are also true.

Sometimes and sometimes

Sometimes I can write freely,
But sometimes it's hard.
Though I do this daily,
Some words I had to discard.

Sometimes I know what to say,
But that's only sometimes.
Though words fill up my days,
Some words just never rhymes.

But it's okay even when it's not,
Because I'm not giving up.
I could never stop,
I'm looking at the top.

I'm still far from it,
But I'm close enough.
Like I said, I'll never quit,
Even if things do get tough.

So even if sometimes I can't,
I can just try again.
I'll meet every wish I sent,
The only way there is to hold the pen.

M.S. Bernardo

Truly someday

There are bags under my eyes
Yet I still live under the bright blue skies
Believing I'm now away from the lies
I've forgotten about my cries

For dreams I hold dearly in my heart
Creating a life such one of beautiful art
And as I continue to keep on hard
Hoping to meet world's highly reward

So still I stay here
Words I use as my gear
Preventing myself to turn to fear
Saving my heart from possible tears

Belief in hope I'll turn out just fine
Reminding myself this life is mine
So I let my dreams age like wine
Truly someday, brightly I'll shine

Keep going

Because if I stop,
Where will I end up?
So I have to go on,
I'm far from done.

Even if the road gets blurry,
I'll try not to worry.
Even though I know I will,
I'll keep up with the spill.

I'll run with my words,
I'm going for the world.
Even if it sounds impossible,
I won't stay invisible.

I'll keep going,
That's what I'll keep doing.
Because this is what I want,
It's a wish I will grant.

I won't ever stop,
I'll never let myself drop.
I'm doing this for my dream,
I'll quiet down doubt's scream.

Because I've become desperate,
And writing feels like my fate.

M.S. Bernardo

Even if it feels lonely,
I'll keep going for it bravely.

What was, what will

I look around me,
Everything's too loud.
The ground I choose to see,
I hear the chaos shout.

Deeper the ground melts,
I forget who I am to be.
Regret as the world once felt,
No longer I wish to see.

I am here but I don't exist,
I stand alone only with fear.
And as reality always insist,
I show them not my tears.

To satisfy them, I turned my back
Against myself, how bizarre.
It was myself that I attack
Forgetting I'm capable to go far.

So once more I look at me,
I realized I should be loud.
I hold my head high to see,
I am more than what chaos shout.

So I let my cold heart melt,
I remember who I am to be.

M.S. Bernardo

Forgetting about the regrets I've felt,
The dreams now I wish to see.

Listen to me as I exist,
No longer am I filled with fear.
And still life will insist,
Show the world not your tears.

I'll satisfy my heart and myself back,
Reality is just as bizarre.
With the end point of my pen I'll attack,
You'll see me only from afar.

Ninety-nine: Lost, Confused, and Found

A poem a day

A poem a day
Can cure a soul
Every word a poem say
Shoots like an arrow

Healing the pain
And feeling the words
Dancing under the rain
Let's not care about the world

Beautiful art of hers
Lay it down beside your dreams
Smile from the universe
Because of her it seems

M.S. Bernardo

Broken branch

There was a moment in time,
When I lived because I breathe.
Then I found words that rhymes,
With my soul so incomplete.

I stood up and smiled,
But living isn't so easy after all.
Every day felt like I've died,
Even then, I wanted to stop the fall.

So I extended my heart,
I grabbed the closest broken branch,
Turns out I held on art,
This life I've always misjudged.

How wonderful it can be,
How painful it made me feel.
The broken branch made me see,
This broken soul's chance to heal.

Beautiful art

Others wonder why I write,
I simply do because it's what my heart wants,
Because through writing I get to see the light,
It's a wish I lovingly grants.

Some people ask how I write,
I write from my heart.
Write down every word that might,
Anything can become a beautiful art.

Some people won't understand,
Simply because they don't have an open heart.
These words gave me a hand,
When people decided to depart.

The friends I once had,
It was my dreams that stayed.
Even if you think I might be mad,
That's not enough for me to be swayed.

I'm glad I chose myself,
I would've never been enough anyways.
There's a future me I haven't met,
I'll continue to fill up my days.

Following my heart,
And doing what I want,

M.S. Bernardo

My life's a beautiful art,
Something they'll never understand.

Ninety-nine: Lost, Confused, and Found

Untitled #1

The efforts of yesterday that I've been forgetting,
Because of the future I'm not seeing,
Will it still bring me towards myself that is so loving?
Or will I just learn how to keep on lying?

The words I keep inside my heart,
Hoping it'll bring out the best art,
How can I trust it when it's hard?
Why do I only cover up the endless scars?

Will I really be able to let myself fly?
Even when my dreams are so far high?
With the words I keep, I continue to try,
So that I can also live while I cry.

Right now I'm still trying my best,
While also letting myself rest.
Forget all about my mind's tests,
There's no need to be stressed.

Someday, everything will be okay,
I'll say the words I want to say.
So that I won't ever lose my own way,
I'll keep trying to live through every day.

M.S. Bernardo

Wishful blows

Yesterday's gone,
Still I am lost.
Death holding life's gun,
In this road I can't cross.

So I walk along the side,
Of this maze-like life,
Hoping someday I'll no longer hide,
Myself from your knife.

Every wish is a dream,
I make a wishful blow,
God hear me scream,
Let my blood glow.

Once I get there

Once I get there,
Will I see you?
This kind of fate is rare,
I hope it's true.

I was lost for a while,
But I'll get there.
Walking towards you with a smile,
I continue to dare.

If by chance I come late,
You'll wait for me, won't you?
I imagine you at the gate,
Welcoming me with a view.

Slowly I will meet you,
I'll see you with a smile.
I really hope this fate is true,
I'll make it worth my while.

M.S. Bernardo

My enemy's grace

Regrets once filled my heart,
Regrets of being who I am,
But as always, it was my own art,
That brought me hope from the sun.

Wishes kept from deep within,
I'm learning what it means to be me,
Walking this road I've been in,
I'm finally starting to see,

Just what life is about,
But of course, I still come across the shadows,
Lurking behind me are doubts,
I'm dodging its painful arrows.

Feelings I've held inside,
Such secrets held me down,
Time gave way and stepped aside,
Time gave me my own crown.

And I won't forget my enemy's grace,
Its mercy on my head,
This feeling of such embrace,
Living a life out of death.

It's a good day

Keep your thoughts positive,
It's a good day.
The dreams that you believe,
Keep going towards your way.

Forget about what to expect,
Just live up to your heart.
These dreams you have to protect,
Even if you find it hard.

I hope you understand why,
These is all for you.
You always have to try,
You have to get through.

Even when you rest,
It's still a good day.
Know that you've been blessed,
Don't you stray away.

Remember the promises,
Don't leave them broken.
Your heart still listens,
So keep your mind open.

One day we'll get there,
We have to keep trying.

M.S. Bernardo

These dreams we promised to share,
We have to keep flying.

Honest form

Things will turn out okay,
Even when it doesn't feel like it will.
Different days come in different ways,
Survive, that was the deal.

Your pen became a sharp sword,
Be careful, don't you get hurt.
Regrets we can't afford,
Be careful with what you'll blurt.

But then again,
Your words are your honest form.
So I'll tell you to keep the pen,
Show the world the power of your storm.

M.S. Bernardo

Future I want to see

The world isn't black and white
Towards truth we must shed light
Fighting for our tomorrow so bright
Here I am again promising to write

My blood gushes red yet my ink is black
My cold heart will only feel another crack
Because of this world that turned its back
Against me who found my own track

Bright as the blue sky I try to be
Let me show you the future I want to see
A world where even a woman is free
Maybe a world where everyone is happy

And in that world I'll still wear my skin
Forgetting this world I've been in
Give me a chance of a new beginning
Let us live with a future of serene

Of course I was

The idea of poetry
Wasn't something I always had
All I wanted was to be free
From this world that is mad

I never thought I'll take up the pen
And fill the pages with my heart
I was just trying to live, but then
I saw the beauty of this kind of art

The spilled emotions
Made me feel something I can't explain
I decided to cross my own ocean
And decided on my own reign

As this is my life anyways
I might as well decide what I do with it
As I go on, I continue to amaze
Myself with every single little bit

Of course I was scared
Of course I wasn't confident
But for me I had to swear
That this life will be well spent

And so I kept going on
I haven't stopped since then

M.S. Bernardo

Even through the dawn
I will be holding the pen

I'm not gone

Days keep passing
I'm stuck
My dreams leaving
I'm locked

Still I'm pushing
I want to survive
Don't want me grieving
Let me stay alive

My head keeps playing
But I'm not gone
My heart's still dreaming
Maybe I'll see the sun

I want to keep on living
Let me open my eyes
Don't stop me from seeing
But save me from the lies

M.S. Bernardo

Will the world favour me?

I ruined my life by putting things off,
I always thought I will have time,
But life is one long climb,
I need to learn more than to rhyme.

Poetry was the beginning,
But my heart is persistent,
And I can no longer pretend,
I need to achieve what I intend.

Stories within stories,
The words flow flawlessly inside my heart,
Poetry of my own arts,
I have to make it through though it's hard.

Will the world favour me?
I'll keep running until it does,
I'll get there, though not fast,
I'll make something that'll last.

Ninety-nine: Lost, Confused, and Found

I'm late, but it's okay

I'm late,
But it's okay.
If that is my fate,
Then that is the way.

It's okay to frown,
I know life is hard.
But even when you're down,
You know life is art.

Because it is your world,
Follow your own time.
Trust my words,
You'll get there just fine.

M.S. Bernardo

A writer

I can't bear the thought of failure,
Of being stolen my own pleasure,
So every moment I try to treasure,
And every moment, time I endure.

Life is the enemy of my soul,
Time's running away from my goal,
So it was time, from life I stole,
Someday, my soul will again shall be whole.

Word after word is my way,
Leaving out the words maybe I'll say,
And tomorrow will be another day,
For me to survive under the cloud so gray.

I'm more than a warrior and a fighter,
I'm a light that keeps getting brighter,
I'm just a girl who wants something better,
I'm just a girl who longs to be a writer.

I do my best

I do my best
So that one day I can rest
Without regrets in my heart
I don't regret holding onto my art

But I admit that sometimes it doesn't work out
Especially when my head's drowning in doubts
But I do my best anyway
I try my best to get through the day

And that makes me proud
Through silence I became loud
Hidden words coming to light
Written words making me bright

That's worth enough for me
At least there's a dream I can see
The future is mine to take
The future is mine to make

M.S. Bernardo

I'm working on it

There's a ringing pain I feel,
It's all over my body,
I know someday it'll heal,
Once I learn to be happy.

It'll come, that day,
It's the thought of it that keeps me going.
To finally embrace the words I say,
To finally feel my dreams growing.

My time will come,
God's given me a chance too.
I'll feel the warmth of the sun,
My smile will be true.

But the time's not here yet,
I'm working on it,
So that there will be no regrets,
This is the promise my heart greets.

The pen, as always, is kind

Will I make it?
That's always the question.
In front of a blank paper I sit,
Leaving my pen in motion.

I write what comes to mind,
I feel the words pierce through my heart,
But the pen, as always, is kind,
My soul shines through my words' art.

How lucky am I?
To be gifted with such ambition,
So of course, I must try,
I must live out my vision.

Hold the pen and write,
Once finish, start the next one.
That's the way I know I'll see my light,
That's the reason I know I've won.

M.S. Bernardo

Goodbye my old pain

Goodbye my old pain,
I've become tired of your rain,
Don't want to be called insane,
Loving your memory only in vain.

I'm stepping forward into my life,
But still holding my own knife,
Choosing the choice to survive,
Back to myself I'll always arrive.

Smiles will come and go,
But my dreams continue to flow,
Looking forward to my tomorrow,
Hoping to forget yesterday's sorrows.

Okay for me

There's an empty space,
Laid out in front of my eyes,
Not leaving my gaze,
Escaping my lies.

What would happen if I leave?
Oh, but what would happen if I stay?
My heart can't find a reason to believe,
That life isn't meant to be okay.

Too hard to understand,
Got no choice but to try.
No offers of a helping hand,
Alone, that's how I'll fly.

But is that okay for me?
Too upset to be pleased.
Many hearts won't ever see,
What it means to be at peace.

M.S. Bernardo

What a pity

What a pity,
I won't read all the books.
Desperate reality,
We're all bait on a hook.

Different worlds of life,
Yet we exist on a boring one.
Characters barely alive,
It's fiction that had won.

I wish I was like them,
Heroes of their own,
But I'm lost in who I am,
I didn't even notice that I've grown.

Responsibilities of an adult,
I'm still the child I was,
Never saw this an end result,
My own field of dying grass.

Greener is the other side,
But the other side's never mine,
But still, I am who was a child,
So I decide with courage I won't be confined.

I'll own up to my crown,
I'll be brave for my throne,

Ninety-nine: Lost, Confused, and Found

I'm done bringing myself down,
I'm living a life of my own.

M.S. Bernardo

It's okay

"It's okay"
The words I wished to hear,
When I was lost on my way,
During that time I was filled with fear.

"It's okay"
Why couldn't you say it then?
You went on your every day,
Don't you live like that again.

"It's okay"
Simple words that is strong,
Don't you go away,
I understand what's wrong.

"It's okay"
I know it's hard.
I know right now you're swayed,
Don't put down your guard.

"It's okay"
Trust in me.
Listen to what I say,
Someday you'll see.

"It's okay"
I won't let you be alone.

Ninety-nine: Lost, Confused, and Found

Even if it feels gray,
Nothing's written in stone.

Tomorrow

Tomorrow I'll still be here,
I won't let myself go,
I won't succumb to fear,
I'm not done with the growth.

Tomorrow you won't miss me,
I won't ever let a day just go by.
There's too many to see,
It's too early to say goodbye.

Tomorrow my words continue,
My pen won't run out of ink,
Every day is something new,
Life doesn't really happen in a blink.

Tomorrow I'll still have the hope,
Reaching for the stars will never end.
Even if I'm tied with doubt's rope,
I won't ever bend.

Tomorrow I still live,
I'll still continue to dream.
There's a list I want to achieve,
This life is mine to redeem.

I'm proud of myself

Sometimes I look back,
And see how far I've gone.
To me it's still a shock,
That I've got many things done.

The days I never expected,
Still meets my eyes with shine.
The skills I have collected,
I'll proudly call them mine.

Though I was once misled,
I still learned how to ascend.
There are still days ahead,
And I look forward to them.

I learned to love myself,
And so I am proud of who I am.
In my heart I found the strength,
And so I can really say I've won.

M.S. Bernardo

Hope

Hope never left me,
But I thought she's gone,
Her pain I didn't see,
Her pain brought out the sun,

I've always wondered why,
But there was no answer,
She was drowning in my cries,
I should've known better,

It was me she was protecting,
My heart bleeding in blue,
She found me dying,
Hope got me through,

She held me in her embrace,
She saved me in her tears,
She became my own grace,
Hope drowned down my fears.

Ninety-nine: Lost, Confused, and Found

Scars of my happiness

My poems aren't majestic,
They aren't flawless,
But they are made of magic,
Scars of my happiness.

Silence in between lines,
There's chaos up in my head,
These words that can't wait to shine,
I have to try before I end up dead.

I write until my wrist might just snap,
I'll write until my soul runs out,
Falling into my own trap,
I've learned to float on my doubts.

But my poems are magic of my heart,
That's all it needs to be.
My soul and my art,
All of these are me.

M.S. Bernardo

Ninety-nine: Lost, Confused, and Found

Dear reader,

Thank you for taking your time reading my written words. I hope that in some way, these words were able to give some comfort, to be a friend and companion. I wish you all the best, whoever you may be, and as hope goes, I hope you're happy.

M.S. Bernardo

CPSIA information can be obtained
at www.ICGtesting.com
Printed in the USA
BVHW071753250922
647705BV00001B/2